FREQUENCIES

ARTFUL ESSAYS
Volume 4 ~ Spring 2014

TWO DOLLAR RADIO
Books too loud to ignore.

TWO DOLLAR RADIO is a family-run outfit founded in 2005 with the mission to reaffirm the cultural and artistic spirit of the publishing industry.

We aim to do this by presenting bold works of literary merit, each book, individually and collectively, providing a sonic progression that we believe to be too loud to ignore.

Copyright © 2014 by Two Dollar Radio
All rights reserved
ISBN: 978-1-937512-22-4

34: "Portrait of Lee Sherman, Radio City Music Hall, New York, N.Y.," ca. June 1947, William P. Gottlieb Collection (Library of Congress).
84: "Smiley face written in the sky during the inauguration of Governor Bob Martinez," Photographed on January 6, 1987, State Library and Archives of Florida.
Cover and all other illustrations: Created by John Gagliano.

Typeset in Garamond, the best font ever.
Frequencies custom font created by John Gagliano.
Printed in the United States of America.
No portion of this book may be copied or reproduced, with the exception of quotes used in critical essays and reviews, without the written permission of the copyright holder.

TWO DOLLAR RADIO
Books too loud to ignore.
www.TwoDollarRadio.com
twodollar@TwoDollarRadio.com

FREQUENCIES

Artful Essays
Volume 4 ~ Spring 2014

Poverty Pimp: Or, How to Get Ahead by Playing Bones on Skid Row
by Colin Asher 1

Noble Toil
by Charles Hastings 23

Q&A: What was your first concert experience? 35
   Sarah Gerard 36
   Nicholas Rombes 37
   Shane Jones 38
   Jeff Jackson 38
   Anne Marie Wirth Cauchon 39
   Carola Dibbell 40

Jims
by Joshua Mohr 45

Now. Here. Crazy. But. Still.
by Ruth Gila Berger 55

An Exclusive Interview With Shia LaBeouf
by The Editors 85

Real Life in the Heady Days of Dial-Up
by Nathan Knapp 93

Contributors 104
About the Artist 106

POVERTY PIMP

OR, HOW TO GET AHEAD BY PLAYING BONES ON SKID ROW

BY COLIN ASHER

tevenson alley is coming to life. Through the lobby windows of the Seneca Hotel I watch as neighborhood regulars meander toward Rite By liquor, or the hydrant on the corner of Sixth St where crumpled bills are exchanged for styrene bags; the slanted afternoon light grants their weathered faces a tired sort of dignity. It's six-thirty p.m. and a few are dressed as if they might be coming from work, though this is unlikely. As the sunlight that had been bathing the hotel lobby gives way to the unforgiving glow of florescent tubes, I ignore the men I'm sitting with to watch the lazy hustle of the alley. It will be all the way dark soon and when it is the police, through unspoken agreement with the neighborhood's regulars, will stop patrolling and the night will grant permission for the chaos that will undo the day's immeasurably meager accomplishments. But it feels calm now, and watching people in no particular rush to go anywhere, advance any agenda, relaxes me.

The Seneca Hotel anchors San Francisco's skid row, a small and shrinking neighborhood that hugs Sixth St south of Market St. Sixth St was once a strip of mid-range tourist hotels. And then it was a stable working class neighborhood. Its decline has proceeded steadily since. Now nearly every building on the block is a hotel with a name like Winsor, Lawrence, or Hillsdale, where rooms can be rented by the hour, day, week, or month. The Seneca stands out among these because its designer's ambitions were so grand. Its lobby has 20-foot ceilings, and enough floor space to hold formal dances which, I'm told, it once did.

A flight of stairs climbs the south wall, and a wall of windows looks onto Stevenson alley. A stone floor boasts a high polish thanks to the prideful, Pyrrhic efforts of a man who I will only ever know as Mack. Even as bedbugs infest the hotel's rooms, paint peels, tenants shatter doors, rip plaster from walls, and throw themselves from the top floors, Mack continues buffing the floor and bragging about its shine. There are days when the building's failing glory feels like a judgment against all of us inside. But on afternoons like this one, weary from a long day and squinting just right, I swear the Seneca is still regal as the day it was built.

As the alley's lazy-hustle slows, I return from my late-afternoon reverie.

In the middle of the lobby is a folding table, topped by 28 dominoes and a smattering of Styrofoam coffee cups. I am seated at the table with three other men, engaging in what has become a weekly ritual of trash talk and low-stakes competition. It's my move, has been. To compensate for my absence, I come back to the play with bluster.

"You think you're gonna lock it up, you smug bastard—and yeah, I know you probably will—but in the meantime-in-between-time, give me my fifteen points," I say, needling Keith[1], the player who has to follow my move. And slap my tile down with enough force to make the sloppy cross of dominoes set before me shimmy and buck.

---

[1] All names have been changed to protect the identities of the people described.

My trash talk is an incongruous blend of Hip Hop generation bravado and dialect that belongs in the mouth of a man twice my age and born much further south. I picked it up at card games, in bars, and around this table. "You're leaking like a wounded soldier," I might tell a player sacrificing points. "If she won't let me in the front door," I chide anyone trying to block my play, "I'll just go around the side." And so I can't tell whether it's my use of "meantime-in-between-time," or the theatricality of the force I used when I made my play, that makes Keith grin.

"Okay, Babyboy.

"Okay. You'll get your due," he says as he scratches three hatch marks on the slip of paper in front of him, and leans far back to watch the rest of us play ourselves.

I lean back too, oversell my cool, feel my face flush and look toward Keith to see if he notices, if my mimicry is too transparent. Catching myself, I sit upright, check the laugh in my throat and wipe my face of expression.

In a place where most people survive on $17.50 a week, lies are currency and everyone wears a mask, ever changing but always present. I am no different.

Around this table I play at being a tenant. This is my most aspirational role. Lately I want nothing more than to sit in on a game like this and have my presence go unnoticed. To drink burned coffee, gossip, and talk a line of trash that no one will bother to remember in an hour's time.

In the halls, the lobby, and on the block I play at being a heavy, a ridiculous act. I mix-in when fights break out, to keep the peace, but also to show that I can handle the chaos. Once I stood between a woman and the dealer she owed her rent money to. I put some bass in my voice that registered as tenor, and said: "You'll get your money, but not today." Why he didn't laugh in my face, push me aside, and beat his money out of her may be a question he's still pondering.

And upstairs, in an office above the lobby, I play at being a social worker: a tragic-comic role. Unlike the other people around the table, I am not a resident of the Seneca. I work here, as a case manager hired by a nonprofit that was contracted by the city to provide social services; a poorly paid, unqualified representative of the city's welfare bureaucracy.

I began working at the Seneca a year and a half ago, and when I did I believed in my job the way one believes in a cause. The city of San Francisco uses the Seneca—along with scores of other hotels—to house the city's formerly homeless population. Working here, I told myself, would be the most effective way I could help the poor. My faith has been dying by degrees since the first day. I have seen people beg for a room on the promise that it is a step up the ladder of stability, but I have seen precious few leave of their own volition. And I have begun to think that the building itself is part of the problem. It is a character in its own right, a thing with its own priorities and agendas that distills and amplifies the many flaws of its residents. And possesses mass and inertia sufficient to drag all of us inside down with it.

The Seneca is six floors of frayed nerves and lottery dreams that sing with praise, growl reproach, and bank prayers like legal tender. Nearly 100 years old, its 210 rooms are arranged above the lobby along three long hallways that parallel each other like

My trash talk is an incongruous blend of Hip Hop generation bravado and dialect that belongs in the mouth of a man twice my age and born much further south.

the tines of a fork. Each one is about ten feet by ten feet. These are small canvases for the psyche, but what the living spaces lack in square footage they make up in pathos: A light mist of dried blood on a wall by the head of a mattress, arterial spray from a shaky-handed injection. Walls that speak to the sleepless through the night as mice traverse pipe and beam and brush against plaster walls. A door only slightly thicker than plywood, just enough security to keep out the honest, and no protection from the sounds of all-night commerce in the hall. A window that looks upon an air shaft, from which you can watch a dozen of your fellow sinners bathed in the glow of TV screens; watch as they bring their profiles into relief with the flicker of a lighter kissing the end of a glass tube, and again, and again. They watch you work your lighter as well. A few months at the Seneca and many start longing for a smaller room, forget the window, and make the walls good and thick.

The role my employer expects me to play in the building is that of a professional. I am expected to remain aloof. Though I would like to call many in the building "friend," I am expected to say "client." It's a small linguistic distinction, but an important one. A tenant might have a legitimate complaint, but when you're dealing with a client you know who the fault lies with. The cause of their trouble is the thing binding them here, their condition. The job, as my coworkers and I discovered, was to identify and name that thing. And so the angry tenants became "borderline," those who ended the day with a beer were "alcoholics," the quiet ones were "depressive" or maybe "dysthymic," and the excitable ones became "bipolar." For every one a label: explanation, excuse, and absolution all in one.

I accepted that mandate with the zeal of a true believer.

For my first year I didn't inhabit the building so much as pass through it. I restricted myself to "Sir" and "Ma'am" when speaking with tenants, and didn't tell them a thing about myself, especially when they asked. Distant, I had been told, was a synonym for professional.

But cracks in my faith appeared early, and spread quickly. It was just so rarely true that people were trapped in the building as the result of some jumble of pathologies.

As a rule, the explanations were far more prosaic: Fired after hurting themselves at work and missing a day to visit a doctor. Then, kicked out of the hotel. Got a job on a cruise ship but the city—happy to pay rent in perpetuity—won't pay for the passport it requires. Been working part time for the school district for five years but can't get on full time. Worked under-the-table for forty years, and received in gratitude a bad back and no social security contributions. Eighteen, kicked out of the house, never had a job, nowhere else to go.

"To insert devise in my body and in my eye micro leans camera, video, tracking devise, wire tap inside my ears," read a note slipped under my door one morning, "…withdrawing blood out of me with needle is a violation of my permission." Here the chasm between what the building promises and what it delivers is widest, because when a tenant truly is troubled we do even less for them. The note's author was evicted for the protection of the other tenants. Another man, in the throes of a lengthy manic episode that had him sleeping in a tub overflowing with water, painting his body in broad stripes as if for war, and swinging from the fire escape while chanting in a language of his own invention, was evicted soon after. And when a longtime methamphetamine addict got clean in jail and asked for a drug treatment program, it took two weeks to find one with a three week wait list. His dealer found him first.

After a year of watching the building's tenants linger in their rooms, their lives never improving and only occasionally becoming more miserable, I realized the Seneca is not a step up the social ladder; it is a stasis machine of Rube Goldberg complexity.

And mine is not a zealot's job. I am not a savior of broken people or a class warrior. I am a bureaucrat: A distributor of government-labeled food and repeatedly-copied Salvation Army clothing vouchers, useful mostly for harassing less sympathetic bureaucrats.

And when I realized that, I started this game, stopped referring to the tenants as clients, and began interacting with them as people.

It seemed the only human thing to do.

The play moves around the table a couple times. Keith takes two moves without scoring off my lead, and it's coming back around when Paul, room 429, places a clammy gray hand on my shoulder. He opens his bloodshot eyes wide in alarm, and says he needs to speak privately. I excuse myself from the table and we talk in hushed voices.

"My jewels," he moans, casting furtive sidelong glances about the room. "Someone has taken my jewels. I had some very, very valuable pieces. And now they're *gone*." The last word comes out in a pleading whisper.

The first time I'd heard about Paul's jewels I'd been alarmed. I should have insisted the door to his room—recently kicked in by the fire department—be fixed immediately. Was I culpable, I'd wondered, and how would I convince the police to take a report from a man who refused to change out of his bathrobe? I had called my supervisor, fearing for my job, and she'd laughed, maybe reading my tone as exasperation rather than fear. "He's talking about his jewels again," she'd said. "What next?" And had changed the subject.

Now I find it hard to believe I was ever that naïve, and tell Paul, as if speaking to a child, "I'm so very, very sorry. Come to my office later and I'll help you file a police report." I say this because I know he will forget the conversation the moment he walks away. But before he stops wagging his head sadly, I finish, "You know... when the doctor told you to drink lots of fluids, that's not what he meant." Here I point to the plastic bottle of vodka hanging by his side. He laughs a weak, coquettish laugh, and shambles away looking, with his long gray hair, beard, dancer's erect posture, and tattered white bathrobe, like the illegitimate, depressive son of a British royal.

The game waited for me but there was no real need. Keith has calculated what tiles everyone is likely to be holding and it's only a matter of time before he locks up the board. Once he does that, all that's left is counting his points, calling the game, and requesting another. I'm on autopilot now, playing well enough to make certain I don't embarrass myself, but not caring beyond that.

Across the table Auri grips his tiles as if they might abscond—"his" this week, other weeks I will have to remember to say "hers"; it's very difficult to keep up—and to my left Garry tries to cheat sloppily by twisting his tiles as he places them to signal what he still has in his hand. Neither knows the game is already over, and I push back from the table to show my disinterest.

Keith is a dominologist, as near a perfect player as I can imagine. And that's about all I can say about him for certain. When he arrived six months ago he told me he had recently returned from Japan, where he spent many years and still had a family and an impressive job awaiting his return. He was here, he said, to care for his mother. When I asked how he ended up receiving General Assistance he demurred, saying something about "family drama" or how it was only for a few months, or saving money. He may have provided all three answers at different points, I can't honestly remember.

I am preoccupied by the process of patterning my adult life. I keep a collection of archetypes in my head, people I might want to become, based upon a long line of mentors who didn't know they were mentors. People whose lives I have sketched and whose characteristics I mimic in a manner I think of as strategic. At the Seneca, Keith is chief among these. Enigmatic, intelligent without formal education, and seemingly untroubled by concerns such as money or status, he is the type of man I have long thought I wanted to be. Around the table I mimic his speech and pattern of play, though I'm nowhere near as talented, and if I'm being honest, I feel lucky, even special, when I'm in his company. He has that much charisma. In the face of any question, no matter how challenging, he is capable of summoning a smile of such beguiling power that it becomes impossible to refute the next thing out of his mouth. But here I say "thought I wanted to be" because I've been watching him for six months now and I can already sense that the half-life of his charm is approaching.

Since arriving his decline has, like the Seneca's, been steady. He has lost some of his cool but none of the braggadocio, and one without the other is a terribly hard sell. I got him a job interview recently, nothing fancy, but a check nonetheless. And when his would-be supervisor—my current supervisor—asked what he expected to be doing in a year he responded:

"What's your position?

"In a year I could have your job."

The greasy swill served by Tenderloin soup kitchens and the junk food that Rite By sells have rounded his figure and swollen his face. The knowing glimmer in his eye has turned to a glaze, and when I ask about his family, or why he doesn't return to them, his replies sound thin and over-dramatized. I curse his imperiousness under my breath, but I can't escape the thought that, in another place, with a new suit, if he was a different color, the man could talk his way into a million dollars.

I do not pretend that this game benefits the tenants. And neither has dropping my clinical facade. I began my tenure at the Seneca with grand notions, but that time has passed. The beneficiary in both instances, is me. When I began acknowledging the tenants' humanity and dropped the pretense of professionalism I was able to see myself and my potential futures in the hotel. I am Keith sinking, Paul treading water, and Mack swelling with pride after successfully plugging a rat hole with steel wool. I am being pulled toward something I could insinuate myself into with such ease that it feels like destiny.

Beneath the masks I wear in the building and on the block hide a few irrefutable facts: I dropped out of high school at fifteen and never went back, leaving me with less education than most of the Seneca's residents. And before accepting this position I had been a bike messenger, and a truck driver, stocked shelves and worked in a bar. My primary qualification for the position I now hold was the six months I spent working the night shift at a runaway youth shelter. I drink more than most of the tenants referred to as alcoholics in weekly case management meetings with my coworkers, at least I do now that I work here.

I have noticed in the last few months that the receptacle of my evening drink keeps growing. It was a tumbler, and then a pint glass. I drink my gin & tonics from a Mason jar now, and near the bottom of one a few days back a memory snuck up on me. I was a child, seated on a plastic chair beside my mother across the desk from her welfare worker. She was requesting money to

In the face of any question, no matter how challenging, he is capable of summoning a smile of such beguiling power that it becomes impossible to refute the next thing out of his mouth.

pay a bill, maybe the lights, maybe the gas, can't remember, and I was crying. As if on cue.

My mother made her case with the reasoned stoicism that is her permanent state of existence in my mind.

Her case worker, intransigent.

I found myself wondering: How did I move from one side of the desk to the other? Why did it ever seem like a good idea? And how easy will it be for me to make the return trip?

As easy as a few years and a couple bad decisions, I figured: easy.

And I have to conclude that the most important thing separating me from the tenants is this: I work here, and they live here.

It's dark now. The lobby is filling, and a small crowd is gathered around the table, which I placed directly in the line of sight from the main entrance. The lobby is protected by a ceiling-height cage whose door swings open at the touch of a button behind the front desk; another set of bars protects the outside door that opens onto the sidewalk; the space between them is a cage and it's not uncommon for people to be trapped inside. That's not a problem at the moment though, because both gates are being held open, defeating their purpose. The desk clerk hollers at strangers as they pass, telling them they need to sign the register, but it's impossible to remember exactly which two hundred plus people live here, and no one pays the desk any mind. Tenants approach me on their way in or out of the building. Most tap my shoulder or cough lightly for my attention, but a few holler from across the lobby and confide their darkest secrets to the room.

As the game winds down I pay half my attention to the play and half to requests made by tenants passing through the lobby. *I need your phone, I got cut off my GA, Social Security denied me again, My case is on next week and I'm going away for a while, You gotta call my doctor... someone stole my Oxys again, You got any food in your office? They say the Sheriff's gonna put me out next Wednesday.* The more desperate a tenant's need, the more casual their approach and nonchalant their attitude: As if every dire outcome had already been inscribed in stone, but the possibility of talking me out of five pounds of USDA rice, or a box of plastic straws, was still lingering out there, worth fighting for.

I finish second in points, far behind Keith who wins again after locking up the board. When I rise to leave the table my pockets are stuffed with a potpourri of scribbled notes and appointment slips; there is a number written on my palm whose origin I can't recall. And as I round the first bend of the hotel's main staircase, tugging on its rickety brown railing when I turn the corner, a figure passes in a blur, mumbling a question I can't decipher.

Above the lobby rooms are packed in tightly. Some units are

occupied in name only. The residents of these rooms are so accustomed to living rough, under a highway overpass, down by Mission Creek or in Golden Gate Park, that they only use their space for storage. Other rooms are stacked with the bodies of friends of friends of friends, of anyone willing to trade a handle of vodka or a microwave dinner for a sliver of floor space. A few rooms are neatly painted, well kept, neurotically ordered by people who leave them only when necessary. Bedbugs are stacked so thick in one room that, at first glance, it looks like mold is climbing from behind the mattress toward the ceiling. Once I entered a room just after an eviction and I could see the wall studs and the sub-floor, thick with dried spilled paint. The room had been deconstructed by its tenant, its skin peeled away and tossed out the window in pieces small enough that we never noticed. But most are somewhere in between: Sad, unremarkable, greasy little caves that stink like frustration and malaise, last month's dirty laundry and yesterday's church basement dinner.

 I pass a dozen of these to reach my office, and pray as I move down the hallway that no one pops their head out from behind a door to make a request.

 In my office I empty my pockets and sort the notes I find, trying to remember which crisis belongs to which room, but I don't rush. I have nowhere to be this evening.

 My office is a converted room, one floor above the lobby and a bit nicer than average. It has a bathroom and two windows, one looks onto Sixth St, the other Stevenson alley. My sorting finished, I sit in the dark so no one thinks to knock and listen to the hotel, the street, and the alley. I can hear feet clomping up the stairs, tenants yelling from one floor to the next, cars honking and men whistling to women from the lowered windows of slow-moving vehicles. The hotel always gets a little wild at this point of the day. During the one evening a week I stay late I feel like part of the lawlessness, the collective energy that grows in buildings like this, swelling floor by floor as calls echo, cash trades hands, deals are brokered, debts are settled, and everything but secrets and enmities forgotten. I feel like part of the angry, loose-limbed freedom allowed those nothing is expected of, the vapor-thin liberty that is the only payoff for living in this kind of dense, manufactured poverty; but in truth I'm a voyeur listening to the echoes of a neighbor's party.

 A bin of condoms hangs from the outside of my office door, and someone has just plunged their hand in and taken a fistful. Mary's door opens, just outside my own, and I can hear her babble as she walks past. Mary is the only person I have ever known who I sometimes fail to think of as a person. I have not met anyone yet who knows how long she has lived in the hotel, or where she lived before. Asking her would be useless, because she does not talk so much as produce an undulating sound that reminds me of listening to an angry debate taking place a hundred yards away. I often lean toward her in an attempt to decipher her meaning, and receive a smile and a spray of spittle before she turns and wobbles off.

 Mary is tall, and walks in an off-kilter way that makes me think she eats fistfuls of muscle relaxants in place of meals, and for all I know she may. I do know that she has a drawer full of bottles in her room, but not because she told me. Mike, one of my favorite tenants, an old-time heroin addict with 40 years worth of stories about falling off building ledges in pursuit of a stash, or smuggling dope into Quentin, told me so. In one of his frequent, chemically loosened, confessional moods he said that he had, for several years, been fucking Mary every time he only had ten dollars to spend on sex. This ended not long ago, when he noticed dozens of pill bottles in an open dresser drawer and assumed this was evidence that Mary had HIV.

"I hope you were using condoms," I chided.

"You might as well smash my dick with a hammer," he shot back.

Most people in the hotel have theories about Mary, and the most common is that she isn't crazy at all, that she is only pretending to ensure that she will continue receiving disability checks. "She's just fakin' it; she ain't crazy," is the repose that follows Mary through the hotel, and though I don't believe it I can understand its source. A few less skilled actors have tried and failed at what they believe Mary has accomplished, and they are jealous. To some, the contrast between their perception of Mary's insanity and the reality of her capacity to survive in this place is just too much to accept. But for others it's just keen observation. As incomprehensible as Mary usually is, she is prone to sporadic bursts of lucidity. Once she stopped at the threshold of my office and declared in a clear voice, "Those motherfuckers took my children. They took my damn kids." And then walked away. After a fight in the lobby, while nerves were still raw and people were milling around, unable to slow their adrenaline, Mary walked through the crowd unperturbed and declared, "You're all trippin'. Just stop it. Stop it!"

As a nonsensical figure who sometimes speaks the clearest truths, I have recently begun referring to Mary as "The Fool," in reference to *King Lear*. I call Paul, the drunk with the missing jewels, "Lear" because the curriculum of City College's English 1B course is the current extent of my serious literary references. It will be years before I understand how pretentious this must seem to my better-educated coworkers. That it marks me as an outsider who wants in, a striver. And shows that acknowledging the similarities I have to the hotel's tenants had a twin effect: It both collapsed the distance between us and contrasted our trajectories. The Seneca has taken plenty from many of them, but it gave me a great gift. It taught me that striving to be seen as enigmatic and untroubled is a fine goal, but credentials are the only insurance against flagging charm. And my first move after the revelation *there but for the grace of God go I*, was not doubling-down on the elements of my biography that drew the tenants and me together, it was enrolling in night classes.

In a few months I will leave this place not as a high school dropout but as a community college student on my way to university. Within four years I will have an undergraduate degree, and a master's degree from an Ivy League school. And I will be the only person during my tenure at the hotel whose accomplishments came as a result of and not despite their time on skid row.

Cars race south on Sixth St, toward the I-280 on-ramp, the bridge, and suburban homes. As the last suit flees the last downtown office building, Sixth St flickers to life in pawn shop neon, the soft glow falling from unshaded windows, and the Morse Code punctuation of flickering lighters. Lazy hoarse-throated cat calls and sidewalk pleas for peace fade beneath the din of the street, and aside and above the fray I watch as hip slummers turn off Market. They travel in packs like animals, for protection against what they won't say (for fear of offending), and try to loosen their limbs for the block it takes them to reach the Arrow Bar.

"Leaches," I spit, "fucking rich kids," but the epithet falls flat.

"So you're a poverty pimp now," a former friend recently demanded of me. And I sputtered defensively, saying something vague enough to hide the fact that I had, miraculously, never heard the term. Poverty Pimp. It feels a little harsh but it's beginning to fit. I wouldn't waste time cursing people who couldn't hear me if I didn't see a bit of myself in them. There's a touch of their clownish mock shamble in my retreat to this office, my self-conscious contemplation, the slope-shouldered walk I'll adopt only until I clear Sixth St, the fact that, though I feel like I belong here, I live elsewhere.

"Tourists," I say, but this rings hollow as well.

What am I if not passing through?

NOBLE TOIL

BY Charles Hastings

o clocks. No windows. No smiles.

I look at the metal benches lining the side room of the labor pool, the thin white walls, and it could be the early hour agitating me but I can't help to think of all the men and women I went to high school with. What are those intellectually tranquil dolts doing now?

Senior year, one by one like flies into the summer blue bug light, they announced their acceptance letters to various universities. They glowed up and down the halls, teeth beaming like lightning before the thunder of the shared news. Everyone shared their enthusiasm. High fives and squeals were exchanged with a final shush and hush from the teachers. *I'm excited for you, but this is a classroom. So keep it down*, they'd say. Time went on and the flies stacked up from the burn of the summer blue. Then the school year ended; off they went and here I stayed. When you're young and dumb you've got the gumption to look at the long line of success education proposes for writers and artists and scoff at it. A special few of us can even say, *Piss on the house that built great minds, I want my own tool shed*. I did and here I am. There they are. My tool shed is the search for noble toil at twenty-six. Apparently I'm in for the long haul; a master's degree in gab and toil.

I bet those flies are not involved in a mandatory five a.m. attendance for the simple possibility to be clocked in any time from six to six-thirty a.m. For an hour and a half I sit waiting for the labor pool officer to assign me to my department. In that hour and half, all I've got is time. The time before, the real time of now, and the time you foresee in the non-palpable future that I may or may not have. After forty minutes she struts out of her office, picks up the sign-in sheets for the various departments, and walks to the front of the room where the horde of temps sit waiting, like being closer to the entrance will gain them favor. She yells out names in Spanish, some Guatemalan dialect, and then a few English names; stopping to answer calls from different departments phoning her for more temps and I sit all doe-eyed, but lookin' tuff like I don't give a fuck who the dodgeball team captains pick.

I've only been working here for a month and already I'm comparing my experiences to the more vulnerable and scared moments of my preteens. Yes, it is this disheartening.

Moments like this morning I think of a young, clean version of my father, unworn or pigeon-holed by the tools laid at his feet, a few feathers of spite roosting in his foliage but overall still drunk on the first light of a new day. I think about when he turned, noticing all the hinges on the rooms, the strings tugging at those around him, guiding their loose hands and aimless careers. I think of the exactness of the cold mechanisms he may have seen in the proposal of a straight-living world and made a choice, violent means and crime. Bustin' windows and cracking dashes for car stereos, then on to armed bank robbery in Oklahoma and eventually peaking at murder one faired as more of a noble toil then just plain old surviving in the great American spiritual maze of grunt work, minimal pay for a commitment of your entire body, all your effort, all your dopey hopes and wettest dreams, your first born, the soul of your dog or cat, and the memory of your first-loved toy as a child. All you're allowed to leave with is the salt deposits from dried sweat in your shirt 'cause like creativity, it is a useless artifact man ejects freely, without request from a superior.

Hard work setup for men like him and me is a trap. A construct of due time respect that is disrespectful, in a true light, to one's self. Imagine the extreme metaphor of a slaughter line, heavy social fences on either side, all funneling to an eventual end, troughs of promises and assurance of prosperity intravenously distributed for the instance when our necks loosen and curiosity peaks, keeping us all moving along, and at the end of this cattle hall, the end to the end-all-be-all culmination of years of trepidation is the final sliding of the blade of futility across the throat of our ambition. The construct was built because one fact was known and is still in principle a fact today. Hungry men, desperate and unsure whether money is made in the wallets or between the ass cheeks of rich men, are malleable men. But it's never spoken of in the small boroughs of government housing or the trailer parks on the outskirts of southern towns where I grew up. Suburban misdirects drown in the faith of their spot in the slaughter line and they hate smart mouths with big questions.

In the end, there is really no one to blame. No face to the construct. I can't make my stand here at five a.m. This poor labor manager had nothing to do with who is the gears in the faceless industrial infrastructure and who is the pig eating at the troughs in the offices above. That is the brilliant part of it. You take one part hungry man, free to suggestion because of

Hastings 27

circumstance; one part civility and the golden rule; and you have a generation of cattle, bulls hornless and cows dried and spade.

There's a chance I'm giving too much leeway for my father's interior monologue when he chose to do his first crime at seventeen, stealing back a car reported stolen after he paid the previous owner in full without receiving a title, but I like to think there is truth in all proposals. If it is a probability then it must exist somewhere in the folds of validity. Maybe young workers care to think nothing of it. My coworkers willfully give a nod and a firm handshake to the trivial men with inflated titles working above them, spite ambiguity of purpose and lack of sound reasoning in the product of those men. And that truly gives way to mental malnutrition, moments of me in the smoke area thinking of placing a warm gun to the temple of men training me to load and work their machines while they watch, men who bear no fruit, men with bounty and no toil as opposed to the dead hump of earning a lowly wage in a competitive atmosphere.

My brain dances when the digital clock finally shows six a.m. Names are called; men and women leave their seats, walk through the metal detectors, are searched by guards, and disappear around the corner. More names are called; men and women, Guatemalans, Mexicans, African-Americans, and Caucasians hop up at the chance to earn their wage. A few look back with sympathy at the rest of us staring at our feet or toeing at the grocery bag holding our lunch we prepared for our non-day of work.

I've been here since five this morning, but some show up before then and still don't work. There's the lucky forty or so

Hungry men, desperate and unsure whether money is made in the wallets or between the ass cheeks of rich men, are malleable men.

who hear their names bounce back off the large panes of glass surrounding the entrance to the room and then there's twenty or so of us who go on waiting, long faces stacked against the walls, eyes dead and unrested, worried, I'm sure, like me. A day off the check is about forty items erased from a grocery list. A day off the check is one more precious item pawned and lost to my world. A day off work is a day sitting at home, staring at a duct taped computer screen, uninspired to squabble on about the flawed infrastructure.

They run the facility like a GM at a McDonald's would; overstaffing and underpaying, creating a competitive atmosphere that keeps a high turnover rate of employees which leads back to understaffing for the same wage when the work was easier and the hours were less. In that system you have a crew that is assigned to different work areas daily. We all compete for hours, compete for relevance in our ever-changing work stations. Work stations within the different sectors are micro-challenges to the daily assignments muttered over the howl and wail of the beltlines or various machines. You have to show up, then once you're there, you really have to show up. Buckle down and bludgeon your spirits upon the machine you're working.

One day I work in shipping, another day I work in west one, another day I work in west two, another in east, another day I work the grinder, feeding boxes of DVDs onto a beltline that pulls them into an industrial saw machine that cuts the packaging and discs in half so they can't be used freely or pirated by the temps, the full time employees, or any dumpster divers who might have previously worked for the company, knowing what they make in the factory. At the grinder you destroy forty to sixty thousand copies of DVD or Blu-ray titles a day. To the consumer public, over a million dollars worth of usable, undefected products. As I loaded these onto the belt, three at a time, I thought and became enraged at the simple math. *I make minimum wage. This happens every day of the week, destroying thousands of titles. After taxes, I'm paid roughly sixty to seventy dollars for a twelve hour shift of lifting boxes from what seems like an endless line of crates that keep piling up as men in forklifts bring more and more for me to in turn take off the crates and load into this machine. Eight rows stacked high, sixteen boxes per row, thirty DVDs in each box.* Long hours afford me the time to do the math and the ear plugs keep you despondent and disconnected from other workers. The numbers rattle louder and louder, like change in a tin cup, shaken for attention, for the hope of charity or food. As the rattling gets louder, the stiff back that begins at three hours becomes sharp pains, starting above your ass in the small of your back leading up to your shoulder blades and finally wrapping around to your upper arms. Numbers stacking, like the boxes you see accumulating on the other side of the machine, then a forklift drives up, hauls off your work, and you begin again. Once my shift ends, another man comes in and does the same for night shift, pacing at three hour increments till he also has fifteen minutes to get to the break room and back before the machine starts again, asking for more boxes, more DVDs, more of man's trash. This procedure repeated Monday, Tuesday, Wednesday, Thursday, Friday, and Saturday. Only a small portion of the big picture I paint and keep track of in my head, just the destruction of the product.

Only sawed-off Guatemalan and Mexican immigrants work these jobs in the North Alabama area really. Hicks complain about immigrants taking their jobs but these are jobs hicks won't work. It takes another level of hunger to do this for years and years, still chatting and cuttin' up in the break room. It takes a real hunger in your upbringing. They're men and women proud to work no matter what the conditions, including twelve hour shifts for minimum wage. They don't care that once the temp agency wrenches through our checks our income is a good dollar or two below minimum wage. It's capitalism. The "only working" economic system: working over the poor, the underemployed, and the immigrants like a lioness working a wounded gazelle in the hind molars of her mouth.

On days like today when you're left in the room with the other destitute souls and they do the final call, the final blow announcement of, *NO WORK TODAY. SORRY, YOU CAN ALL GO HOME*, which is usually two days of your scheduled work week, they console you with the information that the Madison location is open today. A short fifteen mile drive from the Huntsville location. You can make a thirty mile trip for a ten hour shift, an extra fifty bucks. It is an option for those of us hungry enough to travel, thus diminishing the idea of a fair wage after gas and the hours missed.

I am more than qualified for the jobs I've applied to in Huntsville. But after no call backs or interviews that tailspinned into the final conclusion of another couple of weeks waiting for a call back to further discuss the resume sitting on their desk for the past month, I had to walk my broken, beaten ass into one of the temp agencies conveniently located across the city in or near the communities living below the poverty line. I regret it most mornings. I regret the move, walking into that temp agency, hunger, my decisions, my arrogance, and my lack of humility to get over it. I regret not being able to work and be mindful of that opportunity in itself. Maybe that's just my sheep blood speaking up.

They mean to keep us hungry, lean, and competitive with one another. It's a stab at our constitution of fair wage. They, the infamous conglomo-who-gives-a-fuck, know if they keep stabbing that constitution we'll bleed out and all that will be left are our hunger pains and the bill notices. A young man or woman of a worker's volition knows best, better than most, there are things that outlive all our grandiose ideas of fair and right and liberty and they must always be attended to. Not even death, illness, or a mauling by a pack of bears can keep hunger or notices away.

I'm not sure if the flies drunk on summer blue were right or if the construct of toil is faulty. I am however sure this is life in search of a noble toil.

*What was your first concert experience?*

Sarah Gerard

I discovered Master P and Marilyn Manson when I was twelve. That same year, my parents took me to see Third Eye Blind at the State Theater in downtown St. Petersburg, Florida. It was my first concert, and the first of hundreds of visits to the State Theater. I would see Saves the Day and Bright Eyes at the same venue, the Get Up Kids, Jawbreaker, and myriad other post-punk and emo bands. I'd also find a few boyfriends and smoke a good deal of weed out back in the alley, among other things.

The State Theater is standing room only, and big enough for a mosh pit. Smoking in bars remains legal in Florida, so the likelihood is that you can still smoke inside the State Theater today. My parents had a great time. I suppose I did, too, as well as I could without being able to drink or smoke, or engage in any number of adult activities the State Theater was designed for. Afterward, we bought a poster and waited by the back door so we could meet the band.

As these things go, meeting Stephan Jenkins and his crew was much like meeting any other group of strangers in a dark alley with your parents. We exchanged pleasantries and then he signed my poster, and I walked away not knowing what to feel or what had just transpired in my young body over the last several hours. But that year, I would push the play button on my Sony stereo hundreds of times, and listen to the whir of the CD delivering Jenkins' lispy voice to my tiny, flowered bedroom, decorated with his signed poster.

NICHOLAS ROMBES

My first concert experience was seeing Crystal Gayle and Kenny Rogers perform together at the Masonic Auditorium in Toledo in either 1977 or '78. I was in my mid-teens, and this was the music I listened to and loved then, the sort of music that punk would destroy. There was a Rogers song—"Lucille"—that contained a lyrical reference to a "bar in Toledo" and so he was really warmly welcomed and popular there. It was a great experience, and I had the biggest crush on Crystal Gayle with her beautiful, perfectly straight long black hair that seemed to touch the stage. I was so jealous of Kenny.

SHANE JONES

When I was ten my parents took me to see Billy Idol and Faith No More. I was by far the youngest person there and many people (including a man in full black leather with long black hair) gave me high-fives and called me "little man" throughout the show. My mom, trying to get to the front so I could touch Billy Idol's boot, told a security guard to go fuck himself. My dad covered my eyes when Billy Idol had several naked blow-up dolls and phallic toys on stage. Afterward, walking to the car, I remember witnessing a brawl and the man in full black leather gave me a thumbs up as he walked by. Probably one of my favorite memories from childhood was this concert, my first and most memorable.

JEFF JACKSON

There were shows before it, smaller shows in basements and high school auditoriums, but we thought of this one as our first because it was a big name group in a large venue. You know, a *real* concert. We'd failed to get tickets for Talking Heads the month before, so Andrew bought seats for another group we liked more for their 1970s tunes than their new music: Heart. "Magic Man" and "Barracuda" generated some serious FM hoodoo and Andrew had a crush on Ann Wilson from the videos in heavy rotation. He'd even make excuses for their schlocky power ballads. "She's got to make money like everyone else," he'd say. I don't remember what sort of crowd we were expecting, but I recall being taken aback that everyone else was there for the current hits. The audience was a sea of big hair, spandex tights, and jean jackets. Andrew was further devastated to discover Ann had been using a body double in the videos and looked significantly different in person. We'd come hoping for a hit of rock-and-roll transcendence, but instead we got a bunch of aging pros dutifully cranking out late career hits. As we loitered in the back, I realized I didn't even like Heart very much. I had assumed Andrew's musical taste was better than mine, but this had been a major miscalculation. We both felt a bit sheepish. As the concert wore on, we found ourselves drawn in a bit more. Ann's thunderous voice still sounded strong. In the encore, the band tore through both "Magic Man" and "Barracuda" with some genuine intensity. It was a small moment of redemption, but not enough that we ever told anyone else we were there.

Anne Marie Wirth Cauchon

I was fourteen at my first real concert. The band was Attwenger, an Austrian folk/hip hop duo playing at an underground bar in Vienna, Austria. I was there with my DAD who had just finished his PhD in feminist theory, and my Uncle Geoffrey who is Viennese and, among other things, makes film fakes (suitcases of fake money or tins of Russian caviar, for example). Attwenger uses some old-school instruments like the accordion and their rhymes wordplay Austrian slang. I didn't understand much, but it *was* the first time I saw someone stage dive: the accordion player jumped and tried to crowd surf but the crowd was small, not surfable, and so he just slammed his face on the concrete floor. He was pretty drunk, I think, so he didn't care. We were there for a long time but there wasn't any water so I ended up chugging a soldier of Austrian lager... I've spent years trying to interpret the expression on my dad's face when I did.

Carola Dibbell

Red hair, green dress, Appalachian ballads; possible dulcimer. In my back pages, she's filed under Jean Ritchie. But when I play her records now, Ritchie sounds more political and less mellifluous than the woman I remember edifying a small Greenwich Village audience in the small settlement house theater where I'd already spent more time galumphing around the stage than I ever would watching politely from a fold-up seat. These were the pre-Dylan, folk revival '50s, and I was, what? Nine, ten. I'd never been in a coffee house but knew quite a few traditional songs, many of which I'd learned in that very room under the extremely opinionated tutelage of Helen A. Murphy, spinster with a mission, who single-handedly ran the Greenwich House children's theater, emphasizing the value of immigration for the still substantial Italian and Irish West Village community, and committed to teaching history through song.

I spent pretty much every Saturday of my childhood, most of my Fridays, and some of my Tuesdays on that stage during the school year. Miss M was old-fashioned and had a temper, but her approach was what would now be called child-centered, holistic. We warmed up with weeks of skits and improv before we even found out if we were going to play the mule in "Erie Canal," or one of the seraphim in the miracle drama she adapted to make the Italian mothers happy, or Judah Maccabee or Prometheus or Caveman 2 in that interdenominational extravaganza she pulled out once in a while. The age range was four to sixteen. You could work your way up through roles over the years, starting off as the cherub-in-disguise you would sing to when you got the countess part, in high school. Her masterpiece was *Americana*, American history through song spliced with some pretty good blank verse—kind of a New Deal feeling, though Miss M's politics were a little stuffy despite the anti-bomb climax and the apparently pro-labor "Drill, Ye Tarriers, Drill," which featured forty girls in rhythm tunics deploying eurythmy skills to wield imaginary drills in unison.

There's a thing I used to hear people say about African music—and this was before African pop went global, so they meant tribal music: you can't understand the music except as part of the life. I never could quite get my mind around that. It's still music, isn't it? But the music we learned in that room, and I'm not saying we got very deep inside the life it was extracted from—Appalachian, Native American, gay nineties, plantation slave—it got inside ours. Even if you didn't have the solo and were just sitting in that special way Miss M made us sit to listen to the big girls with the good voices. You were still part of it. These songs no one knew but us, whether we thought they were dumb, like "The Reindeer Song," put in for global representation in the Christmas Chorale, or loved them forever, like "No Shelter for Mary"—and what a beauty that one is, so plain, so mysterious—there was no joy whatever in hearing somebody else do them.

Whoever that was in that green dress, singing what I considered the wrong lyrics to "The Riddle Song" from a stage I thought I owned, it was obviously not her fault if I only felt uncomfortable watching her, even if it was a very special opportunity our parents would not want us to miss. In fact, that was part if not all of the problem. Where's the fun in that? It kills the thing.

For me as a young teen a few years later, too bohemian for Alan Freed, too young to hear jazz in bars, even the folk acts I sometimes caught had lapses of worshipful solemnity or forced jollity that left me confused about my role as audience member, though they were sure looser than classical concerts where everybody waited to cough till the break between movements. When I went to the movies, I could be myself, even while watching dolls in period costumes dancing with extremely unlikely young men. I sometimes wonder if, years later, I felt so at home at CBGB because it brought back those Saturdays at Greenwich House. Whether you were Lucifer or Third Villager, you were part of something. Cool punk, stiff intellectual, bridge and tunnel regular, you belonged. Or it wouldn't have been fun.

The first time I felt all that at a live show? Part of something? Fun? No contest. February 9, 1964, with my two timing boyfriend in a living room in Cambridge, Massachusetts, watching the Beatles on TV.

BY JOSHUA MOHR

riving on acid is underrated. It's not as dangerous as you're thinking. You sort of float down the road. Granted, it's hard not to speed. And staying in your lane is almost impossible. It's a cross between a luge and a magic carpet ride.

Okay, it's probably as dangerous as you're thinking.

I worked at a dive bar down on the Embarcadero, and three other dirt bag employees and me scored a bunch of acid and drove to Reno. Actually, I drove to Reno. On acid. They drank beers and sang along to the radio. We had it on a god awful station that played things like Kenny Loggins' "Footloose" and that became our anthem for the trip.

Downtown in Reno—and I'm using that term loosely—is a super sad stash of diners, casinos, strip clubs, and cowboy bars. Nobody has any fun there. The strippers practically use nicotine patches for pasties.

Our first night was your typical hard drinking/hard drugging/take-no-prisoners bender. It's what we expected the whole weekend to be like, but Anthony got arrested early the next morning. I've never been exactly clear—and I don't think he is either—as to what he was picked up for. One theory was that he was sleeping in the hallway of a hotel we weren't staying at. They frown on such behavior.

So we were killing time the next morning—Jabiz, Ben, and me—waiting for Anthony to be freed from the tank. It was before noon, say 10 a.m. or thereabouts, and we were at a strip club that had a "renowned" buffet so we figured we could kill two birds with one bad idea: see naked ladies and eat at the same time. It didn't seem to bother Jabiz or Ben, chewing their food while smiling at these working women. But I couldn't do it: the acid gave me a weird vein of morality, making it sort of tasteless to eat food in front of the girls. I actually sat in the back of the club with my back to the stage, chewing my food like a good little boy, then joining my friends once I could ogle without worrying if I had prime rib in my teeth.

At a certain point while getting a lap dance, I asked a stripper, "Can you help us get some blow?"

"Sure."

"Here?"

"No," she said, "after my shift."

"When's that?"

"Two hours. I can't leave with a customer or I'll get fired. I'll pick you up around the corner."

I reported back the good news to Jabiz and Ben. This was the kind of thing that could turn a day around. I mean, don't get me wrong, the buffet was good, but some cocaine would make sure we made it through the entire weekend with drinks in our hands.

"We should see if the DJ can play 'Footloose' while the next woman strips," I said.

Both Ben and Jabiz thought that was a stellar idea.

Unfortunately, the DJ didn't have the track. Instead, as a Kenny Loggins' consolation, he offered "Danger Zone" from the *Top Gun* soundtrack. You should have seen this woman dance to "Danger Zone." It was a wonderful sight.

We killed the next two hours with watered down drinks. Then the stripper—I can't remember her name so let's call her Quinn—said I should meet her in ten minutes up the block.

The other thing I can't remember is whether or not Jabiz and Ben came with me. Honestly, I can't remember. All I remember is being in her house alone.

She drove us to one of those prefab complexes out on the edge of town. All the condos washed in beige stucco, front yards just tan gravel. We walked into her house and she vanished into the bedroom, told me to grab a beer and sit in the living room. I heard voices in the back and for the first time I got scared. I didn't know her. I could very easily get robbed. Not that their take would be worth the effort. But still, no one wants to get rolled in Reno.

Now thinking about it, I'm pretty sure Jabiz and Ben were there. I remember laughing with someone, waiting for Quinn to come back. Talking about who knows what, but there was laughter, that I know.

Soon, she returned carrying a baby. A little boy with bright red hair. The same shade that I had as a youngster.

"This is Bobby," she said.

"Who were you talking to?"

She motioned to the baby.

"Where's the sitter?" I said.

"You watch him for a few minutes and I'll go get the blow," Quinn said, handing him over before I had the chance to say anything back. Then she vanished into the backyard, through the sliding glass door, and it was Bobby and me. We stared at

No one wants to get rolled in Reno.

each other. I bounced him on my knee and said, "I'm a friend of your mom's."

Maybe Jabiz and Ben weren't there after all because I don't remember anybody saying any smartass shit when she left Bobby with us, with me. That would have no doubt been a hot topic of desolate conversation.

I held that little boy and thought about all the strange men my mom had left me with over the years. There was this one crazy motherfucker, Jim B. I don't know much about him, really. He was the handyman at the company where my mom was the secretary. He had a hair-trigger mean streak. I saw him wing his coffee cup at a car because the guy cut him off in traffic.

One day in his truck he chomped a cigar and said to me, "You tough?"

I was about ten years old. "Yeah, I'm tough."

"Let's see about that." He told me to place my forearm down on the armrest between us. He placed his forearm right next to mine so they touched. Then he took his lit cigar and laid it down on us, so it was burning both our arms.

"First one to move is soft as a baby's ass," said Jim.

Without any dad around I wanted to impress Jim. I wanted

him to say, "Holy shit, kid, you're chiseled out of rock." But I wasn't tough. I was a ten-year-old faking it. I held my arm there, smelling the burn of his arm hair, our skin, I tried to be as tough as was possible but pretty soon I jerked my arm away and rubbed the spot where the cherry kissed it.

"Toughest in all the land," Jim said, retrieving his cigar and taking some celebratory puffs.

Now that I'm an adult, now that I'm a parent, it's hard to understand why my mom left me with men like Jim. It's easy to simply say she was an alcoholic making bad decisions, and that's true too, but I bet she had no idea about the day Jim burned my arm. I probably didn't mention it to her. Truth was I liked spending time with Jim, even if he scared me. He was a man, a tough man, and no matter how dumb it sounds now, I enjoyed being around him. Yes, he was dangerous but he gave me lots of attention. I was never an afterthought with him. When we spent time together, I was his world. And if you spend enough time being ignored, a burning cigar on your skin isn't such a bad body double for attention.

"Your mom loves you," I said to Bobby, bouncing him some more.

Luckily, I had young sisters. One eleven years younger than me, the other fifteen. Jess and Katy. Technically, they were half sisters—my dad had remarried and started a family he liked more than me—but I never thought of Jess and Katy that way. They were my sisters. They are my sisters. So I was good with babies. But Quinn didn't know that. She didn't care. Or she couldn't care. She needed her cut of the money from selling me an eight ball. She wasn't getting rich working the morning shift at the club.

I don't want to say apathy. Don't want to say malice. Don't want to believe Bobby was left with men like me often. Men looking to score drugs. Score anything Quinn was willing to sell. I don't want to ponder all the Jims that might have sat on this same sofa, whipping out their burning cigars or worse. I don't want to say any of that because Bobby deserves better.

Quinn was back in about twenty minutes, offered me a ride to town and I said I'd rather walk.

"It's eight miles," she said.

"I'll call a taxi."

"They don't come here."

"Why?"

"Just let me drive you," she said.

"Can Bobby come?"

"Of course," Quinn said. "I can't leave him here by himself, right?"

She smirked at me, and I didn't know what her face meant and if I did, I pretended that its meaning was too obtuse to decode.

"Want a bump for the road?" she said.

"Sure."

Bobby played on his blanket while we sniffed gagger rails, the kind of brutal eight inch lines that you almost needed a running start to pack in all that powder.

I immediately hated myself and everything in the whole fucking world.

The car ride back to town was quiet, Quinn and I not talking much, Bobby gurgling in the backseat. That red hair of his—of ours—I stared at it in the rearview, knowing that in a couple minutes I'd never see the boy again. He'd live his life and I'd live mine but in this wicked world our paths would never converge.

Sometimes, toward a movie's conclusion a couple quick sentences motored up the screen telling the audience where this man or woman ended up down the line. And I'd like to do the same thing for Bobby. I'd like to cook up a future for him.

First, his mom gets clean.

Second, they get out of Reno.

Third, she falls in love with a good man and Bobby has a father figure. Someone who's never even smoked a cigar.

Fourth, this father raises Bobby as his own, teaching him to be kind, to be a hard worker, to honor his commitments.

Fifth, I want Bobby to never even try booze and drugs, swear them off just because he knows the havoc they wreaked in his mom's life before she got sober.

Sixth, Bobby is safe and solid. He is a safe and solid man with a safe and solid life.

That's what I want so badly for that innocent boy.

And who knows? Maybe that's what happened.

All I can tell you for sure is that they drove off. I was alone in the motel parking lot with the blow. Anthony was probably out of jail by then. Jabiz and Ben were antsy to get high. Bobby was gone, leaving all us Jims in the rearview.

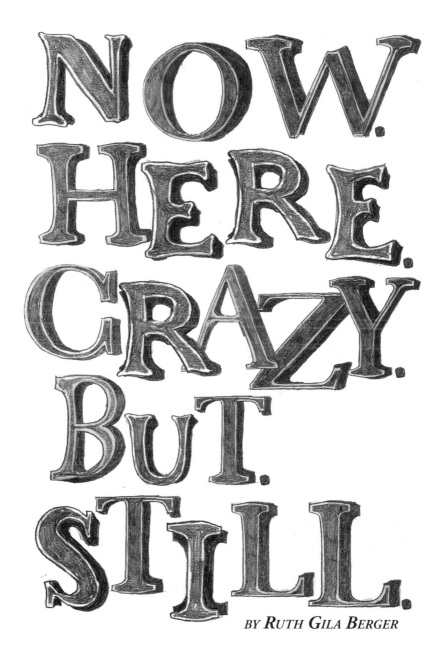

NOW. HERE. CRAZY. BUT. STILL.

BY RUTH GILA BERGER

t forty-one the map of my life offers only a strange coastline of what I might have imagined. For a child often accused of daydreaming it seems odd to me I remember so few of them, my *what do you want to be?* kind of dreams. One was I'd live dining glamorously on a low table with tasseled pillows on the floor for sitting cross-legged. My table would be covered in red silk with gem candles burning late. In my bedroom now the walls pulse around me and I replay the extended task of painting them. First, three coats of a red I misjudged, too pinky-magenta. The second shade was a bit too brown. Staring at the paint in the tray I had laughed. You can't match your bedroom to your lipstick. But then again, I did. Ten years later with a few white nicks the walls please me still. So the map of what I drew young and the map of how I live now coexist oddly. The land and water fit together but the sand holds a ghost of cliff or rock.

As far back as I remember children were not part of my plan. At five when my friends played house I was never the mother, the big sister, or the baby. I tied a black sash around my waist and veered around them on my hands and knees mewing. Like my cat I'd bonk my head into their calves and they'd pet me. The sash was fancy velvet and eventually got ruined trailing the floor behind my feet.

At some point in my twenties I began to say when I'm rich and famous I'll take in a bunch of kids, something like that, maybe. I had no idea what I meant. I still don't, not really.

Right now in August (at forty-one) it means I hear the rumblings of a twenty-year-old as he tries on outfits, talks on the phone, or plays video games in our spare bedroom. He's the second kid to move in with Christi and me. A kid with a history, in a program to give queer youth experiencing homelessness at least a year of stability. As much as we are able we are their hosts. We are not foster parents and although we say we are not looking for a magical instant family, I wonder if in some way deep down I may be. Perhaps we model a version of adulthood for these youth, in that our relationship combines passion and mutuality, an absence of anger, threats, and violence.

The thought we are a model of anything is completely fucking crazy. The first time we heard about this program was through an email, not long after Christi got out of treatment, maybe a year. We were not far past that crisis.

When Christi hooked up with her ex, Gina, Gina's son was four and Christi has been involved in raising that kid ever since. After a night out with him, now seventeen, Christi strides into our room and paces, elbows and knees, angles cracking. Through the surrounding windows the orange winter night filters in. The red walls glow darkly.

Christi's voice jerks, "There's just no going back from this shit. Shut up, kid, Dzzt. I don't want to hear it."

Christi cuts her head off with her hand.

"Dzzt! So I pick the kid up at a friend's house across from his father's, right? And he starts telling me they flipped these two girls and see? It sucks if you fuck the one better than your friend did because and I don't want to hear it. All the years I've tried to teach him. First, about respect and about condoms, Jesus. He came back after his first high school health class and told me I did a shitty job—I didn't tell him about the tip—afterward to pull on it. Like I'm supposed to be teaching him this shit. His father wouldn't. That's fucking gratitude."

I giggle.

Christi's blue eyes blink.

"When we first dated Gina was carless, schlepping him around by bus. Second time I pick them up the kid asks *if you die will my mom get your car?* in this tiny little voice. It was so cute. I should have known. The kid was six the year we had him full-time. It was the year of Neurotin. They tell you specifically not to drink. Whatever. So every night when I was crazy by seven-thirty, sack of potatoes, thunk, out, Gina would shake me and I'd literally crawl to bed. You could tell by my knees, a scraped-up bruisy mess. That's not any way to raise a kid," Christi says.

"Oh honey," I cluck. "Honey, you can't think."

"How did I end up the one to give sex education?" Christi asks. "When he was five he got a sore on his penis and started screaming. I had to come see. He was so worried. Do I have to go to the doctor? Will I have to have a shot in it? No. His father never taught him how to properly clean his penis. Mr. Weekend Warrior off in Kosovo, Jesus. How useless. So there I was with the bacitracin. When his mother got home she went over the steps with him but seriously. Like I'm supposed to be the adult, again? No one else would do the sex talk with him. So there you go, the schizo ex, now that's a great choice. I mean the tip? What was I supposed to do, use a banana? A dildo?" Christi asks.

Voices from the street filter in. We are quiet. A sigh, mine or Christi's, as she settles down to take off her sneakers. She doesn't loosen the tongues to ease them off like usual. She bends down and yanks from the heel, leaving the laces tied. The move seems violent.

"Yeah," I say. "Least he's..."

My voice drops. The world tilts.

"Fuck."

A blank second passes, everything blank. Then I launch from the bed, a spasm of energy—unexpected in the winter when eight feels like midnight—bouncing to turn on the brighter dresser light. On the dresser there are bank receipts and to-do lists I crumple. With a quick arm jut I throw them. The papers make a *kathhh* unfurling by the trash. Missing my target brings bile to my throat, a flood of saliva, a strange taste the Ativan I chewed makes chalky. It's over twenty years but my limbs remember being seventeen, being laughed at. There's a buzz to my skin. Like there's rattlesnakes under it. It's hard to stay present, hearing that rattle. I click my tongue, prophylactic against further noise. The mirror stays me. In it I recognize my reflection. The brown thermal I wear is disappearing in age, a distracted lace; holes bloom from the elbows up the sleeves. I pick at a thread then turn right to flex my triceps. In the mirror my nipples show through the thinning cloth.

"There's something wrong there, with the girls," I say. "Not that they're sluts. That's not what I mean. Or that they're doing anything wrong. Girls are sexual at that age. Why shouldn't they have crazy experiences? Just the atmosphere isn't ready. High school hasn't changed. Girls police. Fuck, at that age," I say.

Reflected in the mirror Christi fuzzes around the edges. Regardless I feel her watching me.

"Because the next day at school is always the same. Neyah-neyah-neyah in the hall. It's a fucked up way to learn about people. That girls can be cunty? An attitude I hate, just to clarify. It takes years to unlearn that shit, that other women aren't bitches. Compete, compete. It's bullshit but no one tells you and then it's almost too late. But by seventeen I was hanging out with lawyers, three times my age. High school was beside the point. Senior year there wasn't anyone older to fool around with anyway. What am I saying? That's not a solution I'd advocate. My point? I don't know my point. What I'm saying is. Two boys have an experience like that and keep it secret? Right. With cell phones, Facebook, bam. That bad shit is instant. For girls who get into those situations, it's not always consensual, not really," I say.

"I can't think about the kid raping someone," Christi says.

"No. That's not what I mean. Nothing about him. I mean the girls. Their history, what got them there. To that situation, getting flipped or whatever the fuck they call it. Look. It would be great to think those girls were there for the sheer joy of it, some wild, crazy fucking. But

Does the falling sand know something of what danced there before it was simply eroded?

remembering, I just don't see the possibility. The culture hasn't evolved. Look at Facebook. It's all cruelty. We've gone back to, Bitch, lock your knees and, Well, you dress slutty anyway. You know? Fuck, I'm sorry. I'm so totally not helping. You talk to me and I'm not comforting. Just I think about myself at that age; I worry. About the girls, is what I mean," I say.

What I don't know. If there's been some interference with the girls' ability to understand their cells. A narrative interrupted doesn't form in the same way neurologically, is vulnerable to influence. Consensual, nonconsensual, without violence to point to, for me, there's a question about what's really understood and conscious. Fillet out the capricious, hair tossed seconds, separate the lust from the story, the understanding of self as agent. I remember myself at that age and worry. What does consent mean? Can behavior serve as evidence of that initial violation?

Every grain of sand holds an echo of rock and cliff. The Palisades on the Hudson by where I grew up tell their own story. Do they hold some bit of soul from each person who died against them? Is there a thrum beneath the rock face that in an earthquake might also be unleashed, an opera built over centuries of battles and murders and suicides and accidents? Does the falling sand know something of what danced there before it was simply eroded? Historical markers do not tell these stories. If every grain of sand holds a ghost of rock and cliff, what happens when it's turned to glass? Can atrocity leave a wobble, an imperfection that cannot be explained? What about a very small bad thing? In a windowpane, a window, in the eye, is it possible that aberration can be seen? In my eyes, is there anything there, any story to see?

There were no historical markers I set for myself. The question that haunts me is more a taunt. Why aren't you over it? When are you going to get over it? It being the thing that happened in my childhood with my grandmother's pedophile husband. How can I be so sure there was something when I don't know what it was? For a girl, now a woman who has or could have everything, why am I still so frozen, so fucked up, so angry?

It is hard to look back. Just, I think about myself at that age; I worry. About the girls, is what I mean.

Picture me, a spectacularly obnoxious teen. My sweaters fall off my shoulders, my necklines gape, I lean forward and shake my hair out deliberately. It is hair that is thin, ratty, brittle, and dry. It is not hair anyone would look at and want to breed for their centuries. I'm a girl boys go with, not one they date. The ones with girlfriends at school who judge me, they think themselves sly. It was not for them I stay quiet but the information they provide. Those boys show me how the girls they cheat on don't kiss. I forget the boys; they are all mostly the same. It is the girls I memorize; their freckles, faded eyeshadow, cheerleader panties, and boring short jeans. The therapist my parents send me to worries I will opt out of the decision on my virginity. He worries I will be drunk, I will be high, I will be in the sky, I will abdicate and I do. It is not the violent scenario he fears for me but one where we are both drunk. I am tripping and laughing, grinding and bucking without what would likely be a virgin's usual inhibitions. The man I'm with is old enough to know what to do with a new woman's body. Funny how I still remember it as great.

It is hard to look back, to look into the hurricane in which we spun. The eye where everything is still? A myth. There is no logic to those historic shattering winds. I have the same questions as everyone.

Why am I here? What am I doing? Does it have any meaning? With no children will there be anyone to remember me?

My experience should tell me, if I know anything, it is this, that we can only comprehend one blink's worth of our own motivations. The rattlesnakes under my skin buzz. One new note in that fearsome song can obliterate all my previous understanding. Now, here, crazy, but. How did Christi and I decide to become involved in a program where we'd take in a strange kid, one with a history we will only know the museum version of, the one that they decide to expose for display, is a hard question to answer. Certainly we've had conversations about children. When we started dating it was about how I didn't like kids. There are pictures of the first time I met Gina's son at a birthday party. In them I look not just uncomfortable but pained. Like my face is a foreign galaxy, a collage I can't quite arrange, click-click flash, I'm forever captured in that state.

Maybe the first conversation about children was when (Christi's friend) Tara was still pregnant and about to have her baby. She asked Christi if we'd be her daughter's godparents. Christi asked me and for a moment I considered it. Certain words are a spiderweb. The baby's father was the younger brother of an ex of Christi's, Lindsay. To say that their relationship had been nearly fatal for Christi would not be an exaggeration. Any connection to her ex was a risk, one neither of us was keen on taking. All rational analysis dictated no should be my only answer. No was my answer when I was a young woman about to get married myself. I told Greg that even broaching the subject of kids could be a deal breaker. While he said that was okay, now I wonder. If we'd lived our lives as intended I would have deprived him of what is now a primary source of joy, the two children he's had since. With Christi I didn't want the power to define things either way.

What I remember of our conversation about being godparents was at my backdoor, both of us paused in digging for keys. I told Christi it wasn't a decision for me to make. If this was something she truly wanted, I'd be there, yes. Christi answered she'd already told Tara we couldn't do it. Three years later both the baby's parents were dead. Tara's baby went to her family, where a happy life was something Christi and I found difficult to imagine. What did our abdication mean?

Certainly our ideas of godparents, gleaned from the romantic stories we read from previous centuries as children were not accurate. The legal fact is godparents are not next in line in the event a child is orphaned. Sometimes facts have nothing to do with reality, the gut level punch of it. On the one hand we dodged a bullet. That Christi went to the hospital, went to treatment and cut off contact with Tara was part of what saved her life. Had we all stayed involved, I don't know that either Christi or I would have survived, our relationship would have certainly become a casualty. The level of maintenance our own sanity then required left no room for a baby needing gentleness, love, and stability. One of the key components to managing a schizophrenic brain beyond no drugs interfering with brain chemistry is sleep, regular, deep, and uninterrupted. So on one hand, we dodged a bullet. On the other was the idea, however inaccurate, that we had sacrificed this baby, the suspicion that our lives went on because she wasn't in them.

That feeling of sacrifice is a familiar hurricane for me, broaching a conversation with my father that had been my entire life in the making. It might be out of order in this story. I'm pretty sure that conversation happened after we got clean because there were no pills to take the edge off after it ended. The exchange comes back to life per chance I catch the drawing Christi did of my father during that visit. It rests against the mirror in our dining room buffet, held up by a dusty bottle of absinthe. Around the picture is an abandoned country of things, magazines,

paperclips, decorations, things, a disturbing accumulation that assaults me. The portrait is in ink and as Christi captured him, my father is young looking; his cheekbones are razors. Her lines provide a personal archeology. It was July, he was wearing short shirtsleeves. At the time he had one objection, one stray vanity.
"I have that little hair? Really?"

Staring from the page, his face is not in its usual configuration. His gaze is clear-eyed, benevolent, even. One lid does not squint twitching, like I've taken something from him, like his life, although his thought would never be that mean or cliché. His glare would state his soul was a recipe and I'd taken the baking powder, altering chemistry and ability. There are times I catch myself focused in the same way, staring into space, scanning the distance for thieves. I am Sméagol now, in a way.

My precious. You stole it.

"Daddy?" I begin. "I need to ask about something. See. I have this memory. I don't know how to do this. I mean memory can be misleading. Will you listen? I mean will you help me?"

I pause.

"You've always backed me on Ray. Why?"

Silence. All my intentions of light conversation, of asking my father about his early life, if he ever had an outfit he wouldn't get out of, or about his first proud lie, vanish. Eyes narrowed, I lean forward.

"Just don't tell me it's because I'm your daughter. What I'm talking about, things are more complicated. People don't just believe those kinds of accusations. Even the well-meaning. What I'm saying is that belief isn't automatic," I say. "That kind of belief doesn't just go with being related."

"But you are my daughter," my father says. "I was there."

"Yeah, yeah. I popped out. Mom said Ruth instead of naming me Sarah. I know. Her big rebellion against tradition. I've heard the story. It's disgusting," I say.

"Not disgusting," he grins.

"Whatever," I say. "What I need to know is. Did you see something? I mean, did you catch him at anything?"

My father's gaze is hard and unblinking.

"You were NEVER a liar," he says.

"I don't know that," I say. "What I need. Did you ever actually catch him doing something?"

"No," he says.

"Nothing. So how do you know?" I ask. "How can you know I'm not lying, making up a story just to have something extreme. Stories. Kids make up stories. And you have to admit I was always a little extreme."

"Because I do. Something happened," my father says. "He hurt you."

"How do you know? What I'm asking for. Evidence. I need evidence. To know something. To give it a name. What you don't understand is everything in my life is a story. I've made up stories to answer this. I need something real," I say. "Otherwise it's all just fucking stories. And I don't know anything. I watch my breath to know I'm real. You don't understand that."

My father interrupts.

His glare would state his soul was a recipe and I'd taken the baking powder, altering chemistry and ability.

"SOMETHING HAPPENED. Ruth, I don't know what but I know he did. He hurt you. I didn't see but you haven't lied."

Holding on to the door frame I look down and reel. My feet, when in focus, are fascinating, suddenly fascinating, the chipped polish crags and peaks of metallic green, they scream.

"But you didn't?" I ask.

I jut my chin and my father drops his head.

"We didn't know then, didn't realize," he says. "That was much later."

"But I have this memory. I've always understood it to mean you did. Know something, that is," I say, fading.

"Tell me," he says.

"It's like this weird collection of images. Picture me, I remember my bangs were crooked and I'm underneath the dining room table, the dark and wobbly one I think later you broke. You're all talking above me where I'm playing. Gladys and Ray are over. Was I three? Four? Five, maybe? I remember watching for their car. But I don't know if it was the Peugeot or the one before that. There was forsythia so it had to be spring, right? Spring? Mom was cooking only I didn't want to eat it. Lamb or tongue, dinner was gross and soapy smelling so I had crackers under the table but the conversation was strange, the rhythm of it, like it was biblical. Only you don't read the Bible. It was before Waldorf School so how could I even know what the Bible would sound like?" I ask.

The cracks on my father's hands are white. Despite the heat his fingers are purplish and when he lifts them from the table I can see his dehydration, fleshy pads indented from where they pressed against the wood. I don't wait for an answer.

"But it was biblical. Like a story of the whale that swallowed Jonah for masturbating. I know that's not right but that's what I want to say it was, what I remember. There was something sexual and it was about me. Then you were yelling. The table was wobbly. You kicked Ray and Gladys out. There was the door slamming. But no one ever explained anything to me. Just a blip. Nothing changed. I always took that to mean you knew something, that you kicked Ray out because you did," I say.

My father's eyes follow my eyes to his hands. The nails curl at the edges, like mine would if I let them alone, didn't stand vigilant. Even shrunken his thumbs seem large.

When I was little we thumb-wrestled; he let me cheat my elbow wild so sometimes I could win.

He speaks slowly.

"It was spring. I don't remember forsythia but it was before the magnolia. The Jewish calendar changes you know. The dinner was Seder. Why your grandmother held on to Seder is a mystery. She wasn't religious. But there it was. Your mother was a good daughter so holding Seder was what we did. It was the

Haggadah, not the Bible that I was reading. The Haggadah for Passover."

A cat runs down the stairs, his galumphing feet capture me, a moment of interference. One tiny cat like a herd of elephants. I watch him bonk his head into my shins but don't feel it. My legs are made of Styrofoam, my green toenails a million miles away.

When I glance up my father is staring just past my head. The lower rims of his eyes seem to separate, pinker than the last second I'd noticed them. I suck the splinter in my hand and sway, again grabbing the doorframe.

"We didn't know. Or if I knew then, it wasn't consciously. I'd have probably killed him if I did," he says.

A jury would have let you off. His baby girl, they'd say. You'd have been applauded. A hero they'd say.

I shake my head for quiet.

"But you know something happened to me. Was it then?" I ask.

"Ruth."

"There was that time I attacked Ray after dinner at Gladys's in the city. I was eight or nine. Old enough that Gladys had removed the plastic from her furniture. I bit him. Do you remember that?" I ask.

"RUTH."

"Why are you yelling?" I ask.

"I wasn't. Ruth. I'm sorry. I didn't mean," he says.

It takes me a second to understand the silence. I stare out the window beyond where he sits. I can't watch him cry so I can't know for sure that he is.

"I think you were too old for him by then," my father says. "You were a baby, two. That's when. We left you with Gladys for a weekend. You came back a different baby. You were psychotic. You reverted, insisted on nursing. You wouldn't stop screaming. You were a psychotic baby. We didn't know anything, all the reading, the terrible twos they say. You were afraid of hands. Shadows. Things moving. Noise. You were afraid of everything. Hands especially, yours, mine. You had long stopped nursing, that was part of why we were confident to leave you with them. The terrible twos. Everything we read," my father's voice leaves off.

"Dr. Spock?" I ask.

"All of it. They talked about the terrible twos. Ray wasn't in," my father says.

I complete his sentence. "Your imagination."

"NO. We didn't know or have a name for, to even suspect anything," he says.

"No Oprah back then," I say.

"Oprah?" he asks. "Right. No. There was no reason," he says.

"Was it the first time you left me? More than in another room, I mean. Like the first time overnight?" I ask.

"Could be," he says.

"Separation anxiety. See!" I exclaim. "Anxiety's a big thing. Separation anxiety."

"No. NOT in proportion. It took weeks. Months even. You were a completely different baby," my father tells me.

"There would have been evidence. I mean from a grown

man. There was no emergency room. I wasn't ripped open," I say. "I was a baby. A grown man can kill a baby."

"He was professional. Some of these people know what they're doing, leave nothing, get away," my dad says. "He used toys."

I rock forward as my toes grip the floor. My feet look blue. There is a loud bang when I blink against the dots. I look up, only I heard it.

"He gave me dolls. They were bribes. They," I say.

"We found," he stops. Squeezes his eyes.

"A box of Barbies. I know," I say.

"Masturbatory implements," my father continues.

I hold up my hands off the doorway.

Picture me a kid. Under a patchwork quilt in a room with blue flower wallpaper. It is probably turn of the century, the pattern a little degraded, stained and ripped. Why I remember there were certain books on the shelves, why I can see the ones that stuck out for being odd-sized photographically, I don't know. Like every kid I was curious about my body. I stuck things into it, a flag from a parade, the point of a comb, my fingers, a stolen Cross pen. Did other kids do that? And remember it? There were doll limbs in me?

"Ray was how I had Barbies. He gave them to me. Toys. I can't," my voice drops. "I can't talk about this."

My father nods. We are silent. Time passes. When Christi gets home I push her toward the stairs, now an inscrutable Escher painting. The light cuts strange angles. We stumble up to our

The stories I wrapped around me had at least started to change, my map of breadcrumbs home from the city, my coastline built of silt and butterfly wings, glaciers and swamplands drying over centuries.

also newly unfamiliar bedroom. Christi sits on the bed; I curl into her.

"Can we nap now?" I ask, pulling her arm to me. "Will you? Okay, please?"

Christi folds me in, my head to her chest. Going on instinct, she forgets I can't do the head to the heart thing most mammals find such comfort in.

I jerk away, loud-loud rattlesnakes buzzing under my skin. She holds on and I inch back, stacking my hands on her lower ribs before lowering my ear onto them. Christi holds me there tight.

"You're gurgling," I say.

"Hamburger, French fries," Christi whispers. "Your mom took me for lunch. You're probably hungry if you didn't eat, no, yes?"

While the conversation with my father about Ray was decades in the making, imagining it as possible was after I'd met Christi. It was only after I'd been practicing breathing the way she'd been breathing for years. Christi's breathing, a study of impermanence, non-attachment. In and out, nothing is forever.

We make choices about the stories we tell ourselves, the stories we repeat as identity. Hers, an artist. For years mine was one of damage, a shingle I hung out, collecting other girls of the fraught blue hours around me. That had started to change before I met Christi. Many of those relationships grew up to concentrate on healing and survival. (My best friend) Marya and I had been meeting weekly for over a decade by the time Christi entered in. Some of that moving on was due to our realization of our advantages, the privileges we'd not always been conscious of having. The stories I wrapped around me had at least started to change, my map of breadcrumbs home from the city, my coastline built of silt and butterfly wings, glaciers and swamplands drying over centuries. The window glass I look through might have a memory of sand, a ghost of cliff and rock. The conversation with my father had something to do with Christi and my journey toward the host home program within which we would take a queer kid experiencing homelessness in. For me that feeling of having been sacrificed to fulfill my parents' dumb urge to breed had to be put to bed. It was a simplistic, bratty, and inaccurate assessment of my life. Christi and I might have had conversations about giving something back, taking all our close calls and lost friends and packaging them all up as an offering. I don't know about that. As kids, we both had taken the lessons we were given and tossed them sky high in a celebration of shattered glass. Over and over we cut our feet, learning nothing. Would some indecipherable kid really accept any answers we could give? Ultimately it was the resources we had to offer, an empty room, a neutral chance, a place that's safe. If not now, when?

It was December. The first kid who moved in was a slip of a thing. Fey and chocolate-skinned, TJ had heavily lashed doe eyes with weary, weary rattlesnakes buzzing behind them, quickly recognizable to me. In winter, Christi and I often succumb to our faltering bones and crank the heat past seventy. TJ didn't remove his jacket, scarf, hat, and boots for at least two days. When he finally came to dinner in fuzzy socks and PJs cut at his knees we nearly cried. Our house let go of its breath. TJ was marshmallows and razorblades, jumping to hug me one minute, barking at me the next.

"Stay out of my business, lady!"

Questions were swords, drawn and pointed. He'd storm out and return the next day, around four in the morning. We learned little, that he had family in Louisiana, into voodoo. That was important to him. We took TJ to a framily Christmas party and after describing everyone who'd be there we asked for a safeword if he wanted to leave.

"Apple pie."

By the time he said it I'd completely forgotten.

"Sounds good," I said, thinking the traditional Swedish desert we were served was disgusting.

Christi went bug-eyed at me. "Apple pie, apple pie!" she hissed.

TJ wore the Christmas scarf we gave him continuously. As he

was into tarot, black magic, and conjuring, Christi found a pashmina with skulls on it. For New Year's Eve we had wine and cheese and toasted with the sparkling juice he could drink.

"Y'all middle class people drinking wine and cheese," TJ said with something like wonder.

Considering our dinner was to be crab legs and a Caesar salad I made, I shook my head.

"Oh no honey, tonight we pretend we're rich and hope that's what the year brings."

Gray January launched a storm of hammers.

Days after TJ moved in we'd gone over a set of goals and opportunities he was working toward. There was a paid internship at a queer-friendly bikeshop, a nonprofit training stray kids in bicycle mechanics. While TJ wanted to be a nurse, the pay and atmosphere meant more than the mismatched specifics. We encouraged him to call—apologizing for the pester as we did it. The second time he blew up and said he wouldn't. School was more important. Okay, we said. Christi had a friend over to help TJ wade through the already complicated process of financial aid complications. The first thing they found was he'd missed his registration deadline. At the question of what next the kid blew up, leaving till two a.m. the next day, back out before six. The alarm went off each time he went out and came in. We got him a clicker but he'd forget to use it.

There are rules for keeping schizophrenic brain chemistry stable. Quality, uninterrupted sleep is key. Slamming doors, banging around, loud noises, sudden noises, are impossible to avoid completely as we live in a city, but we still try to keep things even, with disruptions at a minimum. A certain amount of routine, meals, meds, conversation, reassurance, structured living helps keep the voices tied back at bay. Police lights can splinter into distinct ions and build an obliterating din. Outside laughter can fracture the current narrative of dinner into shitty grade school humiliation that cannot then be reasoned away. An angry kid shuffling behind a door brings paranoia out to dance a wild ballet.

Next time TJ comes in I follow him, ostensibly to talk about how he was doing, clearly not well, the dishes in the sink, the fact I'd just bought a plane ticket to New York, my dad being in the hospital and me needing to visit. I'd be leaving TJ with Christi. She had noticed a ritual knife when his door was open and wanted me to check it was truly just a toy. I stood in the door until the kid looked up at me. His face raisined and he screamed.

"I'm just in so much pain!"

"Shit, I know kid," I said. "I see."

We sat in the late afternoon dark.

"I'm making dinner. Take a nap. Come down in a bit and eat."

When he did I explained the risotto I made.

"Onions, chicken broth, butter, rice, and cheese. Skip the saffron and you can always eat. Throw in a veggie, a little meat. It's healthy."

"Rice-a-Roni." TJ grinned, ate two huge bowls and made a ridiculous mess.

"Cheaper, actually," I said.

The pretention I was brought up with manners quickly died. Truth is I used my fingers and chewed with my mouth open probably till just before junior high. I was a brat who didn't clean my own dishes until the first time I came home from college. Whatever indignant reaction I might have had about each new thing went all humpty-dumpty on me, a crash course in knowing my own lies.

I'm having breakfast with my parents when Christi calls me. TJ's fucked up. She's picked him up at a crackhouse.

"He nods off talking to me, stumbles to bed then charges back out before morning. I can't sleep. He's not answering my texts. How's your dad?" she asks.

"He's home," I say. "Hang in there. I'll be back in two days."

When my parents ask me what's going on I have a random moment channeling Nancy Reagan.

"TJ's on drugs," I say. "That's a deal breaker, sadly it has to be."

Absurd, considering our history. My eyes close, exhausted by the idea of explaining how his running in and out at night and the alarm going off requires too much story and too much revelation. Drugs would not really be the deal breaker, not exactly. Our list of dead being a vague part of why we joined the host home program: untreated mental illness, poverty, AIDS complications, and addiction. Matt, Jenny, Max, Tara, and Dan. My parents don't know Christi bears such a necklace. There is no easy explanation as to why we are involved, not for my parents' consumption. There isn't anything I can quickly think of that doesn't risk interpretation as an indictment of their parenting way back when.

"I hope things are different from what they seem," I say.

We all nod vaguely and retreat to our morning reading.

Someday when I'm rich and famous, I'll take in a bunch of kids.

When I got back from New York I found Christi more freaked out than crazy. TJ had yelled at her again to stay out of his business and she was pissed.

Come back for dinner, I texted. No doubt you need to eat, smiley face and hugs.

I'll be there, he said.

Days passed. We trolled Facebook for clues as to where his refuge might be.

Not a crackhouse, please? He didn't seem like a crackhead. You'd think we'd recognize that shit. You'd think. He didn't seem. You said that. Yeah, I did.

We found a picture of the Anne Sexton book I had handed him. He pointed to it, the most substantial book on the shelf.

His post New favorite book! made me wish he had kept it with him always. He didn't. Four days went by.

Anne Sexton? Her end came tragically.

First we tried hospitals, then we tried jails. The city of Saint Paul posts all arrests and TJ's was on the bus.

Consider the slinky. Used for divination it's a pretty accurate predictor of how fucked up interpersonal expectations can play out end over end to the bottom. Consider the slinky a self-fulfilling prophecy. It doesn't do all that much as a toy. Bling, bling, bling. Down the stairs a couple times and you lose interest. Give it rainbow colors and maybe each moment it looks different. But the slinky falls end over end to its conclusion.

Neither Christi nor I could have anticipated how much it would hurt us when TJ came back to leave permanently.

"Kid don't know what he wants," his stepfather said.

"Leave me alone! I don't want to talk to you," TJ said.

Given how we'd known TJ a month we only tried again once, then left it alone.

Nine months later I found white sneakers he left. I put them under the stairs out of sight where sadly, they glow. I had no idea how fast I'd be attached and how much I'd want to please. The kid liked hot sauce, we bought five kinds. He asked Christi several times to do an art night and I almost put all his muddy acrylic swirls on the fridge but didn't. Our learning curve was steep and that makes me a little fucked up crazy when I think about it. I mean our not knowing ourselves hurt this slip of a kid. And while kids have nothing but time, I think there's this spiderweb of a window, absolutely critical and ever-changing but short. Short, like TJ held on to less time at nineteen than we have at forty. And there's no way to anticipate what you don't know, the moment's self-awareness leaks away leaving the abdomen a container of empty spaces. I had no concept of how little patience I'd have with dishes in the sink, bites from things in the fridge, paper towels in the toilet. There's just no way to tame all the birds, dogs, and roaches that make up one's feelings. This is a lesson I learn or don't learn, over and over again.

In August our second "kid" moves in.

A kid with a history, he has been living with another host couple. He told us he felt burned by them—how they committed to a year but when that time was done, they were done with him. Christi and I nodded. I wonder how much we gave him our own museum version, two lives carefully crafted to be put on display. We're only a temporary place of safety as he works toward the goal of a single bedroom apartment, all his. Now, here, crazy, but.

Our past is always changing.

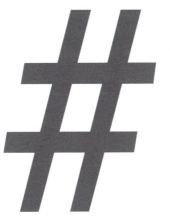 

SATIRE!

"*Shia LaBeouf* **DID NOT** *participate in the interview published herein; the questions and answers are* **fictional.**"

AN EXCLUSIVE INTERVIEW WITH SHIA LABEOUF

BY THE EDITORS

hia LaBeouf made me feel like James Lipton—had Lipton only seen a low fraction of the films that his subject had acted in and was entirely indifferent to those—for the nearly fifteen minutes we conducted our interview at Bob's Bar (tagline: "The Cultural Hub of the Midwest") on a pleasant mid-March afternoon. The beer was cold and the sun shone through the front window onto the initial handful of stools that lined the bar. Shia wore gray and was still missing a tooth. He looked like a distant relative I'd do anything to avoid.

I had never interviewed a celebrity, let alone "the" "celebrity" "of-the-moment." There was a sense that I was witnessing history, while also missing history entirely. Interviewing Shia LaBeouf was like sleeping through an episode of a television show that I really wanted to watch.

In the last four scant months, LaBeouf has dropped anchor in our pool of Eccentric Artists. True, that pool gets pissed in a lot, whether by launching a sketchy rap career or dating Madonna. The point is, this pool makes waves: it is a wave pool.

—*The Editors*

If you could describe your actions in one word, what would that word be?

SHIA: Hashtag, original.

Isn't that two words? Okay then, what about two words?

SHIA: Hashtag, start creating.

Your short film Howard Cantour.com *plagiarized Daniel Clowes, as did the storyboard you posted to your website for* Daniel Boring. *Why are you picking on Clowes, and if you could say 'sorry,' would you say 'sorry'?*

SHIA: I would like to be George Clooney diplomatic. But I mean, I don't give a fuck. At this point I have enough money to live 25 lifetimes. You couldn't spend the money I've accrued now. I have no interest in the materialistic bullshit money can buy. [Other actors are] talking about Ferraris and shit, like it's a cool car. If [someone] pulled up in a Ferrari right now, my idea wouldn't be, 'What a cool fucking guy!' It would be, 'Look at this clown.' I think the fact that I despise that stuff keeps me safe. I hang on to my dirt. I like my dirt. The hardest thing for me is dealing with all this idle time. That's when I get into trouble.

You've gotten into trouble with the law in the past, when you were involved in an altercation in Sherman Oaks, arrested for smoking, and for attacking your neighbor with a knife. What's more fun, punching or getting punched?

SHIA: Dude, I was 185 and ripped. I'm a fucking human being who pays his taxes. And I don't respond in a really sweetheart way. You fight out of fucking survival. Everybody's got stories. I don't want to not have stories.

At your #IAMSORRY show at a tiny gallery in Los Angeles, you had your famous "I Am Not Famous Anymore" bag over your head. Andrew Romano of The Daily Beast *reported that you were simultaneously laughing and crying.*

SHIA: I am trying to impress myself. I have yet to do it.

I thought that was pretty impressive: simultaneously laughing and crying. Not everyone can do that. It's like rubbing your tummy and patting your head. Though the #IAMSORRY piece might appear a bit thin on paper, have you ever considered publishing a show book?

SHIA: I'd feel disgusted with myself. It takes a certain mentality to be able to pay a hooker and stay hard, if you know what I mean. People write books about important shit.

Jaden Smith recently reached out to you in case you "need a fellow insane person to talk to." Most people view your recent actions as performance art. How does that make you feel that he just thinks you're nuts?

SHIA: He's a lunatic. He told me the craziest story at Sundance, about how he used to be a glassblower. He was glassblowing, he said, in his boxers in his garage, and one of the bubbles popped. The glass got on his dick, and it wouldn't get off, because it's like molten lava when it comes off the bubble. He said he went to the hospital and at the hospital they said, "Look, we can't remove the glass because doing so will puncture a vein and then we'll have to sever your penis." So his wife called him "glass dick."

I don't think he has a wife. Jaden Smith is, like, 13.* [*Editor's Note: Jaden Smith is 15 years old.] Do you feel as though he's belittling mental illness?

SHIA: Not like you. No, definitely not. He's a legendary actor.

That might be a tad hyperbolic. We've danced around it a bit, but let's talk about Twitter. It appears to be your new weapon of choice.

SHIA: I don't tweet or do any of that.

Seriously? Every day for a month straight you were tweeting "I AM NOT FAMOUS ANYMORE." Your shenanigans where you claim to want to avoid fame are making you more famous; you're the great celebrity ouroboros. Do you see yourself doing this for the rest of your life?

SHIA: Never wanted to do anything else ever in my life.

REAL LIFE IN THE HEADY DAYS OF DIAL-UP

BY NATHAN KNAPP

1.

I was a firstwave child of the internet. I can still see myself, fourteen, in the bluish light of the desktop screen in my father's tiny home office, typing feverishly, headphones on, trying to cover my tracks so that my parents wouldn't find out what I'd said or who I'd said it to. I wasn't watching porn.

I was chatting.

2.

For most of my childhood I'd been a fairly quiet, self-entertaining kid—I liked to read, could spend hours by myself playing in the woods. With a toy rifle I fought war after war in the woods beyond my backyard, down by the river that flowed green during the winter and died a yellow-algae death in the earth-shattering heat of the Oklahoma summers. In those wars I fought sometimes I won the battle, saved the girl—there was nearly always a girl. Sometimes I died a tragic—but still heroic—death, but only after entreating my imaginary colleagues to keep fighting the good fight. I had free run of the woods, spent hours accumulating sand in my socks and permanently staining my jeans grass-green. When it got hot, I swam, and ran around in dripping swim trunks for hours.

I held onto the imaginary world longer than my friends—I still remember one of our last collective games of "guns," when my best friend Ryan (who was a year older than me) told me he wanted to stop playing because a certain girl named Tiffany was around. He didn't want her to see him participating in a kid's game. ("I have to start thinking about this kind of stuff," I remember him saying, which seems both profoundly sad and eerily prescient to me now.) For another year I held out, unable to give up the world of make-believe, but, increasingly I was alone with my imaginary friends and enemies.

  I remember the last battle I fought: twelve years old, using the front porch as a gun-rest for the last time, getting cold as the October sun went down over the hill, being called in for dinner—realizing the pretend-game was over, probably for good.

3.

I haven't talked with many people about this time of my life, about the fact that all of my best friends during my high school years existed, for me, entirely on the internet. It mystifies me—and for years, has ashamed me—that for a time, my whole world existed in between wires and cables, in code and electric synapses.

4.

I was a young addict—logging onto my email account was for me as big a rush as a gambler making a big bet. That summer hundreds of hours were shuffled into nonexistence as I stared at the screen, whole nights subsumed by my private internet universe, waiting for my friends on MSN Messenger, hoping for a glimpse of the world outside my hometown of Smithville, Oklahoma, which boasts an official population of just over one hundred people. It sits on a particularly lonely stretch of State Highway 259, at the foot of the Kiamichi Mountains, a gentle but steep chain that rests on the southernmost edge of the Ozarks. A remote part of a remote county in a remote state that only makes headlines when it gets destroyed by tornadoes.

5.
I had never encountered a single one of my internet friends in person, most of whom I'd met on a Christian novelist's message board. Naturally, we talked a lot about God. Mostly, though, with the ones that I considered to be my friends, we talked about two things. About writing—and about what *hurt*. We talked about how depressed we felt, about suicide, about hopelessness. Often, we talked about self-mutilation. About wanting to cut ourselves.

Somehow this never struck me as odd.

6.
Not yet having seen *Fargo*, all I knew about Brainerd, Minnesota, was that it was where Genna lived, and that ice fishing was a big deal there.

Not long after we met our internet relationship became the online version of teenage first-love—at least in my case. After a couple of months of internet-only communication, we confirmed each other's actual existences by talking over the phone, and exchanged increasingly long letters, often containing crushed flowers.

In some ways our whole relationship seems precious to me now, ridiculous. But when you're fourteen it seems beautiful to know that someone took four hours out of their life and wrote with real ink on real paper and killed a fucking flower for you. It's so beautiful that your mind latches onto it like it's the one thing that can get you to the last day of high school—a day that seemed impossibly far away to me then.

We schemed repeatedly about contriving some way to meet in real life. But I was too bad a liar and too obedient a kid to actually strike out on my own, to orchestrate something. In some ways I wish I had, if only for the story.

7.

At some point things with Genna turned bad. She told me she liked to burn herself, she told me that sometimes she used a razor on her arm.

I wanted to do something for her. So sincere it hurt, my fourteen-year-old self wanted to save her. But didn't know how.

It hurts to think about now, too. On the one hand, looking over the devastatingly emo pictures I took of myself in the bathroom mirror that summer—sepia tones, black shirts, with expressions as sad and detached as possible—it's hard not to step back with everyone else, point, and laugh. To adults, youth subcultures almost always seem overwrought—and they are. But adults miss the constant *under*wroughtness of adulthood, the stoic underemphasis on the things that actually matter in life.

To the kid wearing that black band shirt, the sepia toned, self-taken photos, all of the semi-manufactured, external trappings of sadness *are* identity, sincerity, significance; the external accessories represent the very real sadness and confusion underneath.

That kid in the subculture invents his own vocabulary, has to do so just to survive.

8.
I was worried about Genna, which, at the time for me was synonymous with being in love with her.

She was a beautiful girl, or at least I thought so, from the snapshots she mailed me in one particularly long letter that August. To my fourteen-year-old eyes, she looked like she felt everything. Something about her all-black clothing, eye shadow, and the general seriousness of her posture and expression, all registered not as melodramatic or manufactured but rather as pain. Real pain.

9.
This is how it is to be a teenager: to feel but not have the words, much less the experience, to give the words meaning.

10.
I even cut myself once, too. It was on a cold January night. I'd been waiting for Genna to come online for months, worried sick from reading her Xanga updates, which seemed to get more morbid with every post. When she appeared, her screen name was illuminated in the happy blue color with the word AVAILABLE in parenthesis alongside. My chest caught, I stopped breathing.

I sent a deluge of messages; she didn't reply except to say she hated me—she didn't care.

With that, she went offline, which was better than nothing

because it meant she was alive—a fact I had been worrying about—but what she'd said hurt my fourteen-year-old heart worse than anything I could have expected.

I took my dull pocketknife out into the yard, into the dark and looked up at the stars. I pressed the knife into the upper side of my wrist, cut a *V*. The *V* stood for my screenname, Voronwë.

The blood on my wrist was a connection, the internet-child version of making a blood pact: It was a way that I could be there with her, with the blood there on her arm in Minnesota.

Upstairs in my room, I opened up a notebook and smeared the blood across one of the pages.

11.
One day in the spring of my fifteenth year—Genna had disappeared from the internet at this point, though she was very much still present in my mind—my father sat me down in his office and tried to explain for me that black was not really a color. That even God didn't mean for us to wear black all the time, as I had been doing.

It wasn't a color, damnit, it wasn't a color.

My father hardly ever swore, but for the color black, and my wearing of it, stronger words were called for.

I contested. He won the argument. And when I say that he won the argument I mean that he and my mother refused to buy me any more black clothes.

12.
Other laws were passed down by parents. During a trip to New Mexico, driving through the mountains south of Taos, my dad told me that I was no longer going to be allowed to go online. Further than that, all of my evil-sounding music was to be taken away. Passive kid that I was, I didn't yell, didn't scream. To be sure, I protested.

Mostly though, I cried like a five-year-old.

Even though I continued reading Genna's Xanga and even made one of my own—which would be later discovered and the contents of which would extract tears from both my parents' eyes—I soon completely lost touch with her.

We wouldn't talk again until I went to college, some three years later.

13.
When we weren't busy venting about how much life sucked we were often talking about writing. All of our talking was writing, in a way. Each line entered into the little blinking box was written in hopes that the person on the other end would respond in kind. And sometimes a hollow, sinking feeling as the other person would fail to reply.

All I was really saying:

Tell me I exist. Tell me I exist. Tell me exist.

14.
As far as I know my parents never found the bloodstained notebook. But they knew something was going wrong with me, just

like I had known something was going wrong with Genna. I remember reading in my mom's journal that she was worried about me, that she didn't know what was wrong with me.

One memory that still pains me to this day: I was stacking firewood between two trees by the dirt road that led to our house, when my dad drove by in his pickup. I didn't even bother to wave at him even though my hands were free and I was standing a mere ten feet from the road.

He stopped the pickup in its tracks about a hundred yards from where I'd been working, reversed it until he was alongside where I stood. He leaned out the window.

You didn't even say hi to me, he said. *I'm your dad*, he said. He was crying.

15.

Genna and I are still in touch—we talk on the phone once or twice a year, like any other pair of old friends who live at opposite ends of the map. As of yet, we've still never encountered each other in person. We're Facebook friends, just like billions of other people around the world. And with the advent of the Manti Te'o scandal—the famous linebacker from Notre Dame who spent four years "dating" a girl who turned out not to be a girl at all—I admit that I'm gratified to know that she verifiably exists.

And maybe one day we'll see each other in person—though it no longer matters so much to me. After all, we've already met in real life.

16.
Every adolescent experiences acute isolation. Then, when many of those adolescents grow up—if they do have to grow up—they see that isolation differently. As I look back over those blood-on-the-wrist poems I wrote, back over those despair-filled journal entries, I can see the melodrama I couldn't during the experience. Like many of us, I make fun of that awkward kid trying to look tragic in the photo, and I give that poor confused creature little credit, give him no forgiveness for his overseriousness, for his maudlin late-night scratchings at the glass of adulthood.

We judge our adolescent selves because experience has given us the privilege of knowing that the world doesn't have to end when our first girlfriend or boyfriend breaks up with us. Experience gives us the knowledge that there are much worse fears ahead. But the privilege of experience is still privilege, and the coruscating light that it shines on the miseries of our adolescences is often as false as it is true.

17.
These days I still sit down and try to write something worthwhile. Sometimes the hollow feeling returns: the suspicion that I'm only speaking to myself. Tell me I exist. Tell me I exist. Tell me I exist.

CONTRIBUTORS

Colin Asher's writing has appeared in nearly two-dozen publications, a few (*The Believer*, *The Los Angeles Review of Books*, *The Boston Globe*) reputable. He wakes up at 4 a.m. every morning to work on a biography of Nelson Algren for W. W. Norton (forthcoming, 2016).

Ruth Gila Berger is excited to be featured in *Frequencies*! This past December she was published in *The Doctor T. J. Eckleburg Review* and had more work this spring in *Permafrost* and *The Writing Disorder*. Her most recent finalist commendation is from *Arts & Letters* for their 2012 nonfiction contest. Prior publications include *Gulf Coast*, *Creative Nonfiction*, *Chelsea Review*, *Water~Stone*, and others. She lives in Minneapolis with her wife and three cats.

Charles Ray Hastings Jr. is a writer and musician born and raised in North Alabama. He's spent the last ten years writing, recording, and touring in the melodic hardcore band, Latin For Truth, and writing for zines and music websites. He's also written various poems, short stories, and essays published through small print and digital publishers Before Sunrise Press, Flaneur(UK), *The Birmingham Arts Journal*, and more. He currently writes for *Valley Planet*.

Nathan Knapp's writing has appeared in or is forthcoming from *The McNeese Review*, V*ol. 1 Brooklyn*, *jmww*, *HTMLgiant*, *elimae*, *Sundog Lit*, and others. He edits *The Collapsar* and lives in Stillwater, Oklahoma, with his large dog, tiny cat, and lovely wife.

Shia LaBeouf is not famous anymore.

Joshua Mohr is the author of the novels *Fight Song*, *Damascus* (described by *The New York Times Book Review* as "Beat-poet cool"), *Termite Parade* (a *New York Times Book Review* 'Editors' Choice'), and *Some Things That Meant the World to Me* (a *San Francisco Chronicl*e bestseller and one of *O, The Oprah Magazine*'s top ten reads of 2009).

About the Artist

John Gagliano is the house-artist for all issues of *Frequencies*, whose original artwork graces each cover of the journal and whose illustrations accompany essays.

He was born in Floral Park, NY, and currently resides in Brooklyn. John completed some four years of art school at FIT and appreciates the fact that he doesn't limit himself to one medium or idea. However, acrylic seems to be his weapon of choice. In 2007 he joined Unruly Heir and fills a momentous role, creating unique prints, T-shirts, and brand illustrations that bestowed another dimension to his commercial work. His art has been shown throughout New York, and many other cities along the east coast. *johngagliano.com*

Also published by TWO DOLLAR RADIO

A QUESTIONABLE SHAPE
A NOVEL BY BENNETT SIMS

* Bard Fiction Prize for 2014
* *The Believer* Book Award Finalist

"[*A Questionable Shape*] is more than just a novel. It is literature. It is life."
—*The Millions*

NOTHING
A NOVEL BY ANNE MARIE WIRTH CAUCHON

"Apocalyptic and psychologically attentive. I was moved."
—Tao Lin, *New York Times Book Review*

"...a riveting first piece of scripture from our newest prophet of misspent youth." —*Paste*

MIRA CORPORA
A NOVEL BY JEFF JACKSON

* *Los Angeles Times* Book Prize Finalist

"Like nothing I've ever read before and is, unquestionably, one of my favorite books published this year." —Laura van den Berg, *Salon*

CRAPALACHIA
A NOVEL BY SCOTT MCCLANAHAN

"[McClanahan] aims to lasso the moon… He is not a writer of half-measures. The man has purpose. This is his symphony, every note designed to resonate, to linger." —*New York Times Book Review*

"*Crapalachia* is the genuine article: intelligent, atmospheric, raucously funny and utterly wrenching. McClanahan joins Daniel Woodrell and Tom Franklin as a master chronicler of backwoods rural America." —*The Washington Post*

Also published by TWO DOLLAR RADIO

HOW TO GET INTO THE TWIN PALMS
A NOVEL BY KAROLINA WACLAWIAK

"One of my favorite books this year." —*The Rumpus*

"Waclawiak's novel reinvents the immigration story."
—*New York Times Book Review*, Editors' Choice

RADIO IRIS
A NOVEL BY ANNE-MARIE KINNEY

"Kinney is a Southern California Camus." —*Los Angeles Magazine*

"[*Radio Iris*] has a dramatic otherworldly payoff that is unexpected and triumphant." —*New York Times Book Review*, Editors' Choice

THE PEOPLE WHO WATCHED HER PASS BY
A NOVEL BY SCOTT BRADFIELD

"Challenging [and] original… A billowy adventure of a book. In a book that supplies few answers, Bradfield's lavish eloquence is the presiding constant." —*New York Times Book Review*

I'M TRYING TO REACH YOU
A NOVEL BY BARBARA BROWNING

* *The Believer* Book Award Finalist

"I think I love this book so much because it contains intimations of the potential of what books can be in the future, and also because it's hilarious." —Emily Gould, *BuzzFeed*

THE ORANGE EATS CREEPS
A NOVEL BY GRACE KRILANOVICH

* National Book Foundation 2010 '5 Under 35' Selection
* *NPR* Best Books of 2010
* *The Believer* Book Award Finalist

"Krilanovich's work will make you believe that new ways of storytelling are still emerging from the margins." —*NPR*